# Back
## from
# Extinction

Written by Joshua Hatch

Flying Start
to Literacy®

T0363503

# Contents

# Introduction

What would you think if you saw a woolly mammoth ambling through an open field? Or spotted a pterodactyl flying overhead? Can you imagine watching a sabre-toothed tiger lounging on a tree limb? One day, you may be able to spot these, and other extinct animals, in real life.

Woolly mammoths became extinct about 4,000 years ago.

An artist's impression of pterodactyls. These flying dinosaurs became extinct about 66 million years ago.

When a species goes extinct, it means every last one of the plants or animals in that species has died and can no longer **reproduce**.

Unfortunately, thousands of plants and animals have gone extinct – many of them because of people. Humans killed so many woolly mammoths, eventually there were none left. But now scientists believe they might be able to resurrect some extinct animals.

The question is, should they?

# Chapter 1

# What is de-extinction?

De-extinction is the science of bringing a species back from extinction. The idea that extinct species could be brought back comes from the science of **DNA**. In every plant or animal's cells, there are special molecules called DNA. These molecules contain all the instructions needed to make the organism. When plants and animals **reproduce**, the DNA tells the **offspring** how to grow.

A scientist examines a DNA molecule. Your DNA molecules contain all the information needed to make you.

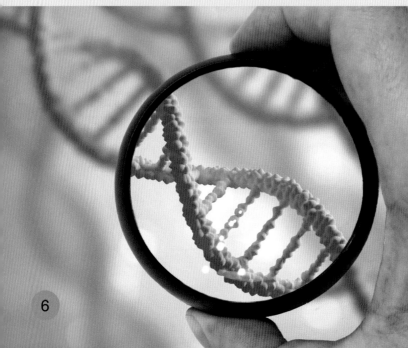

A model of a dinosaur. Scientists know what dinosaurs looked like from bones and fossils they've found.

Scientists believe that if they can control DNA, they could help return extinct species to life. They call this process de-extinction.

For many people, this idea seems crazy – like something from a Hollywood movie. In fact, this idea was used as the plot of a Hollywood movie: *Jurassic Park*! But now the idea might not be so fanciful. Some scientists believe it could become reality.

# Dolly the sheep

One of the reasons scientists believe de-extinction could be possible is thanks to a sheep named Dolly. In 1996, scientists created Dolly by the process of cloning. She was the first mammal to be cloned successfully from adult sheep DNA.

Typically, animal offspring are created when male and female DNA combine during fertilisation of an egg. The combination of some male DNA and some female DNA creates a new **embryo** that grows into a baby. That's why children have some characteristics from their fathers and some from their mothers. They are a combination of both Mum and Dad.

But making a **clone** works differently. With cloning, a new individual is created from the DNA of only one other individual. That's how Dolly the sheep was made.

Dolly the sheep is on display at the National Museum of Scotland.

**To make Dolly:**

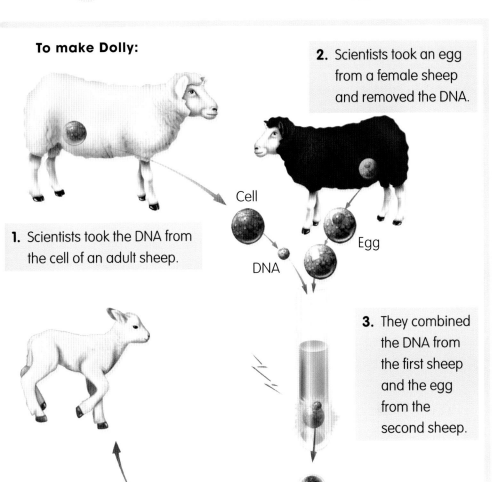

**2.** Scientists took an egg from a female sheep and removed the DNA.

**1.** Scientists took the DNA from the cell of an adult sheep.

Cell

DNA

Egg

**3.** They combined the DNA from the first sheep and the egg from the second sheep.

**5.** Eventually, the female gave birth to a clone of the original sheep. This lamb was Dolly.

**4.** The egg was then implanted in the uterus of a third sheep (female), where it grew.

## Does cloning make de-extinction possible?

Yes, it does! If you have the DNA from just one cell of one animal, then you have the complete set of instructions to make that organism. It's like having a recipe for pancakes. With a recipe, all you have to do is follow the steps – and at the end, you'll have a yummy breakfast!

But there's a problem. With pancakes, if you don't have the right ingredients – or you don't have a frying pan to cook with – you're out of luck. No pancakes for you. Cloning is like that, too.

If you don't have the full set of instructions in the DNA – or you don't have an animal that can turn the egg into an embryo and give birth to a baby – you're not going to be successful.

This starfish has grown four new arms from a single stump. The longer arm is all that remains of the original starfish.

## Clones in nature

Clones aren't just something scientists make. There are clones in nature! If a starfish loses one of its arms, not only can the starfish regrow the arm, but the lost arm can also grow into a new starfish – one that is genetically identical to the original starfish!

# Chapter 2

# What are the challenges of de-extinction?

There are three main challenges to overcome with de-extinction:

- The first is finding **DNA** with enough of the instructions intact that a new organism can be created.

- The second is finding a **surrogate** mother that can carry a fertilised egg to birth.

- The third is making sure the species can survive – after all, it already went extinct once.  Why wouldn't it go extinct again?  To help ensure survival, scientists have to create enough genetically distinct individuals for the species to remain healthy.

A river of ice in the Arctic, where woolly mammoths used to roam

In 1977, a frozen baby woolly mammoth was discovered buried in Arctic ice. This is a plaster cast of that baby woolly mammoth.

## Finding the DNA

For some animals, finding preserved DNA is easy. Hundreds of woolly mammoths have been preserved in the Arctic ice for thousands of years. Keeping DNA frozen is a great way to keep it intact.

But without a living woolly mammoth, where would a new egg come from? What animal could serve as a surrogate mother for the egg, helping it grow so it could eventually be born as a baby mammoth?

# Finding a surrogate mother

It turns out elephants are closely related to mammoths. As a result, scientists think an elephant egg could be injected with the revived mammoth DNA and then inserted into a surrogate mother elephant.

After two years – that's how long it takes a female elephant to go from fertilisation to giving birth – maybe the first mammoth in tens of thousands of years will be born!

Or maybe not. Nobody has ever tried this procedure before. Scientists believe it's possible, but until someone successfully shows that it can be done, it's just a theory.

**How to bring back a woolly mammoth**

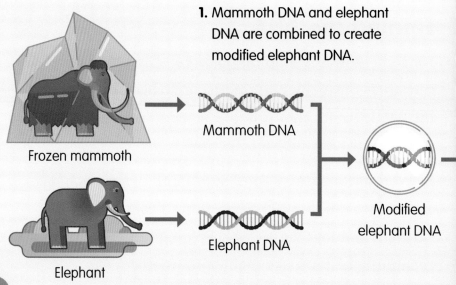

1. Mammoth DNA and elephant DNA are combined to create modified elephant DNA.

Frozen mammoth

Mammoth DNA

Elephant

Elephant DNA

Modified elephant DNA

A baby elephant (left) and a baby mammoth (below) are closely related.

**2.** The modified DNA and egg are combined.

**3.** The egg is implanted in a surrogate female elephant.

**4.** A mammoth-elephant hybrid is created.

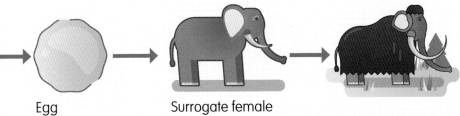

Egg

Surrogate female elephant

## Ensuring survival

But the bigger question is, where would dinosaurs – or other de-extinct animals – live? If we brought pterodactyls back to life, what would they eat? Where would they live? Could people really coexist with these giants hovering overhead?

Answering these questions may be the biggest challenge when it comes to bringing an extinct species back to life.

▲ Pterodactyls became extinct about 66 million years ago. Even if scientists could bring them back, their **habitat** would be so different now that they might not survive.

◀ The Tasmanian tiger became extinct in 1936, more than 80 years ago. It lived in the forests of Tasmania and its habitat still exists.

◀ The woolly mammoth became extinct 4,000 years ago. There are habitats today that are similar to where woolly mammoths used to live, but scientists cannot be sure that they are exactly the same.

# Bring back the dinosaur

So what about dinosaurs? Could they be brought back to life? Could *Jurassic Park* really come true? Chances are, no. Scientists say DNA can't last more than a few hundred thousand years. The last dinosaurs walked the earth 65 million years ago, or 100 times longer than DNA can survive. So it's unlikely we could even recover usable DNA.

Plus, what animal could act as a surrogate mother for a dinosaur? The closest living relatives of the *Tyrannosaurus rex* appear to be animals like ostriches, alligators and chickens. Clearly, those wouldn't work.

### Think about it

There have been five mass extinctions in the earth's history. Each time, at least half of the planet's species were destroyed. Some scientists are worried we're living through a sixth mass extinction.

# Chapter 3

# What causes extinction?

A species becomes extinct when individuals die faster than they can **reproduce**. In some cases, this happens because of some **catastrophic** event. An asteroid slams into the planet, or a volcano erupts, and suddenly all the organisms in the species die.

Other times, extinction comes more slowly. Maybe food sources disappear, new predators arrive or the **habitat** of the species changes. If the species can't adapt quickly enough, it can become extinct.

Scientists believe that a large asteroid hit Earth about 66 million years ago, wiping out the dinosaurs.

Models of the dodo. These birds lived on an island in the Indian Ocean. They were hunted to extinction in 1681.

One of the biggest causes of these changes is humans. We destroy habitats, introduce new predators, compete for food and even kill other species.

Humans weren't responsible for the extinction of dinosaurs – they died out millions of years before the first humans appeared on Earth. But humans are responsible for lots of other extinctions. People hunting woolly mammoths contributed to their extinction thousands of years ago.

# Bring them back!

Some people argue that because people have caused the extinction of some species, then we should try to bring these species back. They say we can undo our past mistakes. They argue de-extinction is the right and **moral** thing to do – if we can do it, we should do it.

Another argument for bringing back extinct species is that we may be able to improve the environment. After all, a habitat is a complex web of interconnected relationships involving living creatures and nonliving things. Remove one piece of the web and the whole system is weakened. But others say habitats are already damaged, and a de-extinct species would have no place to live and no habitat to be a part of.

### Did you know?

The woolly mammoth was just one kind of mammoth. At least a dozen other mammoth species lived around the world. And the woolly mammoth wasn't the only creature with a woolly coat, either. If you could visit Europe several thousand years ago, you might also see a woolly rhinoceros.

A model of a woolly rhinoceros

# Saving species from extinction

Some people disagree with the idea of de-extinction.
They say there are thousands of species in trouble now,
from insects to frogs to elephants. It would be a lot
easier, they say, to save species that still exist rather than
trying to bring back ones that are gone.

These animals are extinct.

Steller's sea cow

Ibex

Great auk

Harlequin toad

# Preventing
# extinction

In 1979, there were between 1.3 million and 3 million elephants in Africa and Asia. As recently as 2019, that estimate is about 440,000. That's a drop of between 65 and 85 per cent. At that rate, elephants could be extinct by 2050, if not earlier. So what can be done to save them?

The most important step is recognising that elephants are in trouble. Then people can take action. Laws make it illegal to hunt most elephants, or to buy ivory, which is made from elephant tusks. There are also efforts to conserve wildlife habitats where the animals, including elephants, can roam free.

Doing this isn't cheap. It costs money to set aside land. But, the cost of extinction is the disappearance of elephants forever.

# Chapter 4

# Bringing plants back from extinction

Plants, not just animals, go extinct.

That's what happened to one plant on on the island of Hawaii in the United States of America over 100 years ago. The Maui mountain hibiscus was known to have a unique scent, but the plant grew only in this one isolated spot on the slopes of a volcano in Hawaii. When the plant died, so did its particular smell. Luckily, a visiting **botanist** had taken cuttings of the flower and preserved them before it died.

The shield volcano Hualalai in the distance, Hawaii, USA

These Maui mountain hibiscus trees grew more than 100 years ago on the slopes of Hualalai, a volcano in Hawaii, USA.

A few years ago, some scientists decided to see if they could resurrect the fragrance, not by bringing the hibiscus back to life but through genetic engineering. Their idea was to extract **DNA** from one of the cuttings and insert it into yeast.

If you've ever made bread, you know yeast can grow quickly – and when they do, they release the strong doughy odour. But this yeast, with the hibiscus DNA inserted, wouldn't make the doughy odour. It would instead re-create the lost smell of the Hawaiian flower.

Sure enough, when the DNA was inserted and the yeast started to grow, the scientists could smell a flower that had gone extinct more than a century earlier. They smelled pine and citrus, sweetness and spice. They had reconstructed a scent from a long-ago time and place.

But why had this plant gone extinct in the first place? It turns out the birds that pollinated the flower had disappeared. Rats ate the seeds. People had destroyed the flower's **habitat**, and caused it to go extinct. If they had taken more care, maybe scientists wouldn't have to engineer yeast to re-create the flower's smell.

## Ancient Greek plants

Ancient Greeks and Egyptians relied on a plant called silphium as perfume and a medicine to treat various diseases. The plant was so important to some old European cultures, it was shown on ancient coins. Unfortunately, the plant was overharvested and died out. It makes you wonder: Are there diseases today that silphium could have cured?

A drawing of the plant silphium

29

# Conclusion

The idea of bringing dinosaurs back from extinction is an exciting one. That's why it was turned into a blockbuster movie. But the reality of de-extinction is far more complicated.

Not only is it incredibly difficult to do, it may not be a good idea. It could be exciting to see woolly mammoths and dinosaurs walk the earth again but shouldn't we instead focus on preventing elephants and other creatures from dying out in the first place? Should we try to recover what we've lost, or prevent more losses from happening at all? What do you think?

# Glossary

**botanist**  a scientist who studies plants

**catastrophic**  having disastrous consequences

**clone**  to make an exact copy of something using the DNA material from one parent

**DNA**  the substance that has genetic information in the cells of plants and animals; it's an abbreviation for deoxyribonucleic acid

**embryo**  the early and developing stage of an animal's offspring

**habitat**  the place where animals and plants grow

**moral**  concerning what is right and good

**offspring**  the young of an animal

**reproduce**  to make babies or the young of animals

**surrogate**  a substitute female person or animal to carry offspring

# Index